VERSAILLES

THE CHÂTEAU, THE GARDENS, THE TRIANONS

Béatrix Saule

Director of the National Museum
of Versailles and Trianon

With the collaboration of

Mathieu da Vinha

Scientific director of the Château
de Versailles research centre

Contents

Historic introduction   7
    The Galerie des Carrosses   13

Visit of State Apartments   15
    The Chapel   16
    The Palace History gallery
    and Louis XIV Rooms   18
    The King's State Apartment   20
    The Grand Gallery   27
    The King's Apartment   32
    The Queen's State Apartment   37
    The History Galleries   44
    The Apartments of the Dauphin and Dauphine   46

Other tours   49
    The King's Small Apartment   50
    The King's Private Cabinets   54
    Marie-Antoinette's Small Apartments   56
    Mesdames' Apartments   59
    The Opera   60
    The History Galleries   62

The Gardens   65
    West Side   66
    North Side   71
    South Side   74
    The Avenues and Groves   78

The Trianon Châteaux
and Marie-Antoinette's Estate   87
    The Grand Trianon   88
    The Petit Trianon   90
    The Queen's Hamlet   92

Timeline   94
Genealogy   95

View from the
Royal Gate of the
Marble Courtyard,
the Château and the
Grand Perspective.

Historic introduction

The cherished memories of his first hunts at Versailles inspired Louis XIII to build an initial hunting lodge there in 1623-1624. But the building was immediately ridiculed. The King then commissioned his architect Philibert Le Roy to undertake reconstruction. Although the end result was bigger, boasting the proportions of a vast lordly residence, it was still far from royal. Despite several modifications by the architect, "the little house of cards", as Saint-Simon dubbed it, remained unchanged until the sovereign's death in 1643. It was also somewhat by chance that the future Louis XIV discovered Versailles for the first time in 1641 since his father sent him there with his brother to escape a smallpox epidemic in Saint-Germain. He was to return as King ten years later to enjoy the pleasures of the hunt. He would henceforth visit regularly for his personal amusement.

Although Louis XIII had a hunting lodge built with its own gardens on the site in the 1630s, it was Louis XIV who truly created Versailles. Removed from the rebellious people of Paris, yet within reach of the city, the site offered plenty of opportunity to build: it thus fulfilled the King's desire to gather his Court around him, something that no other royal residence in the area could offer. It was he who gave the palace its grandeur; it was he who mapped out its destiny. Between 1682 and 1789, with a slight hiatus between 1715 and 1722, Versailles was the seat of the absolute monarchy and became its symbol, since the place itself, modelled according to the Sun King's wishes, reflects the way he conceived power.

The dwelling place of all power

In an absolute monarchy, all power comes from the King. In Versailles, Louis XIV was Master of his own house, just as he was Master of the kingdom that he governed through intermediaries that owed him everything. Excluded from affairs of government, the Nobility no longer held any real power, yet they nonetheless felt the need to appear at Court. It was there that the King dispensed favours: offices, land, titles, pensions, etc. In this society founded on prestige and appearances, emulation was constant, luxury compulsory, life extravagant. In this way, Louis XIV "had a hold" over his courtiers. It was he who had to dominate in every way; in his eyes, the exercise and

Previous double page
View of the Marble Courtyard.

Hyacinthe Rigaud, *Full-length portrait of Louis XIV aged 63 in grand royal costume*, 1702.

Pierre Patel, known as Patel the Father, *View of the Château and gardens of Versailles, from the Avenue de Paris in 1668*, 1668.

outward signs of power were one and the same thing. His residence had to be the biggest and the most beautiful and its décor loaded with symbols to his glory. The number of servants, in the noble sense of the term, assembled in the King's House had to be the greatest and his Court had to be attended by the most people; between 3,000 and 10,000 courtiers, depending on the day. At the end of the reign, the Château itself could host 4,000 residents, while outbuildings in the town housed 2,700. This huge crowd had to be strictly regulated. Etiquette and its constraints may seem pointless to us today. However, protocol was essential, since it served to confirm ranks, the primacy of the King, in short the hierarchy within the Court. It applied to the Sovereign's most private moments such as getting up in the morning, mealtimes and going to bed at night. Another specific feature of Versailles, and something which naturally astonished foreigners, was that both the gardens and the inside of the Château were largely open to the public. Anyone, be they a member of the Court or otherwise, could see the King when he crossed his State Apartments to go to the Chapel. They could even go right into his Bedchamber, as long as he was not there. All these functions – representation, government, accommodation and service – explain the lay-out of the place. But it was not built in a day.

Fifty years of building work

When Louis XIV came to his father's hunting lodge for amusement at the start of his own reign in 1661 and ordered the first alterations, even he could never have imagined that this small building, consisting at the time of the structures that surround the future Marble Courtyard, was to become the core of a vast complex. During this youthful period, he initiated building work inside – entrusted to Charles Le Brun – and outside, initially favouring the extension of the grounds and the gardens, immediately entrusted to André Le Nôtre, which became the setting for festivities so extraordinary that Versailles became known throughout Europe. It was the day after the *Grand Divertissement* festivities of 1668 that the King noted the smallness of the structure and so decided on the first extensions. Le Vau and d'Orbay, the King's architects, enveloped the old Château with three main buildings overlooking the grounds. The new buildings constructed in stone and according to the tastes of the time – a baroque Roman villa style – contrasted so starkly with the brick, stone and slate architecture dating from the time of Louis XIII, that there appeared to be two châteaux, slotted one into the other. Le Brun, Chief Painter to the King, provided the drawings for all the internal décor of the State Apartments and for the sculptures of the fountains with their multiple water effects in the parterres, avenues and groves. Apollo, the Sun God with whom the King was identified, reigned throughout. Between the King's apartment, which extends to the north, and that of the Queen, to the south, the central facade on the garden hosts an Italian-style terrace with a central fountain.

But this new Château no longer sufficed and the arrival on the scene of Jules Hardouin-Mansart greatly modified the physiognomy of the Château allowing it to assume the dimensions we know today. In 1677, this accelerated building work reflected the determination of Louis XIV to move the Court and Government to Versailles permanently. Thus began an immense building project, which, in spite of the tens of thousands of men working on it, was far from complete on 6 May 1682 when the King actually moved in to the "palace still filled with workmen" according to the Provost Marshal. Under the guidance of Hardouin-Mansart, the Château's surface area

Étienne Allegrain, Promenade by Louis XIV with views over the North Parterre in the gardens of Versailles, around 1688.

increased five-fold. As of 1678, the Hall of Mirrors replaced the central terrace on the first floor. The interiors were constantly renovated, the groves continuously redesigned, the water pipe work increasingly ambitious. But wars towards the end of the King's reign hampered the progress of the projects. The fifth and last chapel was only officially opened in 1710, albeit unfinished. It was the King's determination and fifty years of hard work, hesitations, trials and tribulations that ultimately led to the creation of a whole where everything was carefully mastered – both nature and men – where everything was ordered and structured around a line passing through the centre of the royal residence, where the King's bedchamber has been located since 1701.

The constraints of etiquette

On the death of Louis XIV in 1715, the court left Versailles for Vincennes and then Paris. It was the twelve-year-old Louis XV who asked to return to the residence of his great-grandfather in June 1722. The Château had suffered for seven years but this hiatus did not lead to the end of this court "machinery", which had become an attribute of royalty and the life blood of Versailles. Up until 1789, it was imposed on Louis XV then on Louis XVI, no doubt both imprisoned by this burdensome heritage, who were required to reproduce the same customs in the same places as their forefather. Despite being increasingly seen as restrictive, expensive and antiquated, no reforms to etiquette could be made without affecting too many privileges.

Hubert Robert, View of the Green Carpet at Versailles, 1774-1775.

Versailles continued to function in the same way as it had under the Great Monarch, outwardly at least. Unlike Louis XVI who was not a building king, Louis XV perfected the work of his great-grandfather, with this same spirit of magnificence, commissioning the decoration of the Hercules Salon, the Neptune Basin and the Opera. But in addition to this ceremonial life, these sovereigns also led a simple personal life, sparing them from the constraints of etiquette. The fashion was for elegance and privacy. Nooks within the Château, small apartments and private cabinets multiplied, housing a very small circle of family and friends, in décors constantly updated to reflect the tastes of their time. The greatest sophistication was reflected in the décor, the conversation, the music, the food, etc. Kings and Queens too frequently withdrew to their own private apartments or to Trianon. Louis XV, and especially Louis XVI and Marie-Antoinette, adopted this attitude with no heed for the consequences. The courtiers grew tired of it all, wondering "What's the point of coming to Versailles?" On the eve of the Revolution, the Court was often deserted; the nobility had distanced itself from the King.

From the Revolution to the present day

The Revolution emptied the Château of its furnishings but spared the building itself. All of the paintings left for the Louvre Museum and the furniture was sold, with only a few exceptions. The new regime understood the historical and symbolic importance of the site. After years of neglect, it was restored first by Napoleon I, and then by Kings Louis XVIII and Charles X, both brothers of Louis XVI. But none dared make it the seat of power: moving into Versailles would constitute provocation; it would be too suggestive of a return to the Ancien Régime and its privileges. For a while, nobody knew

Jean-Baptiste Martin the Elder, *The Stables viewed from the Château de Versailles*, 1688.

what to do with it and demolition was even considered, but the Château was ultimately saved by King Louis-Philippe. In a spirit of national reconciliation, in 1833, the "King of the French" decided to turn it into a museum, dedicated to "all of France's glories". Opened in 1837, the History Galleries offer a concise representation of France's history in monumental form, from the foundation of the kingdom to modern times.

Several themed rooms – Africa, the Crimea, etc. – were envisaged but not all had been completed by the end of the July Monarchy in 1848. There then followed a period of transition for the palace and Napoleon III, as under the Ancien Régime, used it for numerous parties and receptions during the Second Empire. The advent of the 3rd Republic, after the defeat at Sudan against Prussia, was chaotic and as of 1870 Versailles served as a refuge for the future governmental system. In March 1871, the Opera Royal was fitted out in less than ten days by the architect of the estate and the assembly in order to host ministers, committees and all elected representatives. Parliament sat there until December 1876 when the Congress Room was completed in the south wing, able to accommodate all senators and deputies. It was they who would elect the President of the Republic at Versailles until 1953, from Patrice de Mac Mahon through to René Coty. Alongside the History Museum, since the start of the 20th century, curators and architects have focused on restoring and refurnishing the royal and princely apartments that make up the core of the Château, while adding to the collections of paintings and sculptures that still occupy its wings. The palace crossed eras and endured the threats of wars with works placed in storage, fully demonstrating its central role in the history of France. In fact, during World War One, the Hall of Mirrors accommodated wounded soldiers while the peace treaty ending hostilities was signed there on 28 June 1919. The showcase for French know-how during the Enlightenment, history museum, national palace and symbol of the Republic, Versailles was also the theatre for numerous international events such as the receptions of Queen Elizabeth II in 1957 and the US president John Fitzgerald Kennedy in 1961, as well as the summit of heads of states and governments of the leading industrialised nations (G7) in 1982. More than three and a half centuries after its creation, the estate, despite having lost its hunting grounds, still remains vast, with its three Châteaux, its stables (the Grand Stable now accommodates the Coach Museum), its garden, its park and outbuildings: 830 hectares of grounds, 20 km of roads, the same amount of closing walls, 350,000 trees and as many flowers planted every year, 35 km of water pipes, 13 hectares of roofs, 2,143 windows, 67 staircases...

The Galerie des Carrosses

The Galerie des Carrosses is located in the Grand Stables built by J. Hardouin-Mansart in 1679-1682. It occupies a gallery that has retained its former appearance, its oak panelling with hay racks and its elegant wrought iron lanterns. The carriages on display were assembled by Louis-Philippe. It was thus that Napoleon Ist's wedding party arrived at Versailles on 2 April 1810 in seven ceremonial coaches evoking the splendour of the imperial court at its height. Also on display is Charles X's coronation carriage, designed by the architect Percier for Louis XVIII, but which the latter never dared use in the political context of the recent Restoration. Louis-Philippe also purchased sedan-chairs and sleighs; the latter were already at Versailles under the Ancien Régime when they were used for racing along the snow-covered paths of the grounds or on the frozen Grand Canal. In 1833, Louis XVIII's funeral carriage joined these vehicles; it is the only remaining example of a royal funeral hearse.

Charles X's coronation carriage built in 1821.

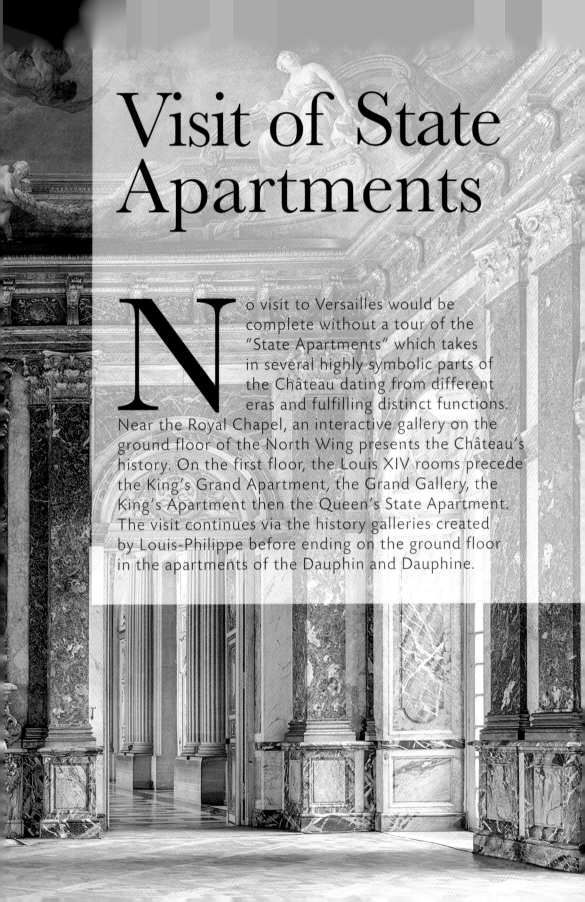

Visit of State Apartments

No visit to Versailles would be complete without a tour of the "State Apartments" which takes in several highly symbolic parts of the Château dating from different eras and fulfilling distinct functions. Near the Royal Chapel, an interactive gallery on the ground floor of the North Wing presents the Château's history. On the first floor, the Louis XIV rooms precede the King's Grand Apartment, the Grand Gallery, the King's Apartment then the Queen's State Apartment. The visit continues via the history galleries created by Louis-Philippe before ending on the ground floor in the apartments of the Dauphin and Dauphine.

The Chapel

Following the tradition of the Palatine chapels, the Chapel has two storeys. The galleries were reserved for the King, the royal family and important members of the Court, while the rest of the congregation occupied the ground floor. Consecrated in 1710, and dedicated to Saint Louis, ancestor and patron saint of the royal family, the chapel was the last building to be constructed at Versailles under the reign of Louis XIV. The decoration of the ceiling depicts the continuity between *Old* and *New Testaments*, with its three constituent paintings referring to the Holy Trinity: in the centre, *The Glory of the Father Announcing the Coming of the Messiah*, by Antoine Coypel; above the altar, *The Resurrection of Christ*, by Charles de La Fosse; and above the Royal Gallery, *The Holy Spirit Descending upon the Virgin and the Apostles*, by Jean Jouvenet. To attend Mass the King had to cross this room, which links the Royal Gallery to the State Apartment. Its decoration is therefore related to that of the chapel, but the themes are more secular; two niches hold statues commissioned by Louis XV: *Glory holding the Medallion of Louis XV*, by Antoine Vassé, and *Royal Magnanimity*, by Jacques Bousseau.

Previous double page
View of the Hercules Drawing Room.

Below
Detail on the pipe organ, *Armes de France portées par des victoires* (French coats of arms carried by victories), gilt wood 1708-1710.

The Palace History gallery and Louis XIV Rooms

The gallery of the Château's history on the ground floor

It is to Louis-Philippe, King of France from 1830 to 1848, that we owe the transformation of Versailles into a museum dedicated to "all of France's glories". Through his desire to reconcile all regimes, the "Citizen King" managed to create the country's first history museum. He turned the apartments of princes and courtiers into vast rooms accommodating ancient sculptures and paintings to vivid effect. In the North Wing, between the Chapel and the Opera, the eleven ground-floor rooms feature a gallery on the Château's history. After a general introduction to the Château and its estate, visitors can discover the main stages of construction since the first Versailles of Louis XIII, the palace of the Sun King, the gardens, changes in the 18th and 19th centuries, through to the Versailles of today. Multimedia rooms facilitate understanding of this transformation of Versailles via its different facets: the hunting lodge, the royal residence, the history museum and the national palace.

Proud of his efforts to save Versailles, Louis-Philippe wanted to be depicted in front of the Château entrance accompanied by his sons. This painting is now on display in the Château's history gallery. Having succeeded in making Versailles a place of memory, he was keen to oversee the work which he funded from his own purse.

The Louis XIV Rooms

Horace Vernet, *Louis-Philippe and his sons in front of the Château de Versailles*, 1846.

The first floor hosts paintings, sculptures and furniture in the palace's collections relating to the Grand Siècle in consonance with the ground-floor gallery. Louis XIV serves as the visit's guiding figure with a number of rooms making biographical reference to the sovereign's childhood and the regency of Anne of Austria; the royal family; assumption of power and the policy of the kingdom; and the court at Versailles. In other rooms, a themed presentation is preferred, structured around the major figures of the "King of War", the "Very Christian King", the "artists of Louis XIV" and the principal royal households and their decorations.

The King's State Apartment

The State Apartment, thus named in contrast to the King's Private Apartments or Private Cabinets, was completed during the construction of the Hall of Mirrors and the War and Peace Drawing Rooms from 1678 to 1686. After having briefly been used as a dwelling for the King, the State Apartment was used both as a ceremonial apartment (some of the finest paintings from the royal collection are hung there) and as reception rooms during what was known as "apartment evenings": these generally took place three times weekly from All Saints' Day through to Easter. Held between six and ten in the evening, they were the setting for the various diversions provided for the courtiers.

The Hercules Drawing Room

This drawing room was built as a setting for Veronese's *Meal at the House of Simon the Pharisee*, a gift to Louis XIV from the Republic of Venice in 1664. Built on the site of the fourth chapel used from 1682 to 1710, hence during the major part of the reign of Louis XIV at Versailles, the Hercules Drawing Room, begun in 1712, was only finished in 1736 with the completion of François Lemoyne's ceiling representing *The Apotheosis of Hercules*.

Veronese, *The Meal at the House of Simon the Pharisee*, 1576.

The Abundance Drawing Room

This drawing room originally gave onto the Cabinet of Curios and Rare Objects (today Louis XIV's Games Room), where were exhibited the most precious items from Louis XIV's collections. According to Mademoiselle de Scudéry, they were "vessels set with gold, with diamonds; others with agates encrusted with emeralds, turquoise, jade, pearls etc., Chinese and Japanese porcelain". Thanks to the balustrade painted around the ceiling by René Antoine Houasse, we have some idea of the items in Louis XIV's rare objects collection. The most marvellous was the nef decorated with diamonds and rubies which held the King's napkin and cutlery, and which is depicted above the door, opposite the windows, surmounted by *Royal Munificence*.

The Venus Drawing Room

On apartment evenings, the Venus Drawing Room was used for the serving of light meals. The *Mercure Galant* reports that tables were set up there spread with silver dishes containing preserves and fresh and crystallised fruit. In addition to the perspectives painted in trompe l'œil and the two statues of Meleager and Atalanta (also in trompe-l'œil), glorification of the sovereign here takes the form of a full-length statue by Jean Warin, representing Louis XIV as a Roman emperor. In the ceiling oval, René-Antoine Houasse painted the subject which gives this Drawing Room its name, *Venus subjugating the Gods and Powers*.

René Antoine Houasse, *Venus subjugating the Gods and Powers*, 1672-1681.

The Diana Drawing Room

Louis XIV, who was an excellent billiard player, had a large table set up here, covered when not in use with a crimson velvet cloth, its edges fringed with gold. The ladies followed the game from benches set up on platforms, which gave them a good view and allowed them to applaud the King's successes. The whole of the decoration of this room refers to the legend of the goddess Diana. Above the fireplace is Charles de La Fosse's *Sacrifice of Iphigenia*, and opposite is *Diana Watching over the Sleeping Endymion* (1672) by Gabriel Blanchard. The room also hosts the bust executed by Bernin during his stay in France in 1665.

Bernin, *Bust of Louis XIV*, 1665.

The Mars Drawing Room

Until 1682, this drawing room was used as a guardroom, which explains the war décor, in particular the cornice decorated alternately with helmets and trophies. It then changed its function, being used for concerts on apartment evenings, and between 1684 and 1750 there were galleries for musicians on either side of the chimney-breast. In the reign of Louis XIV *The Mystic Marriage of Saint Catherine* by Veronese hung above the fireplace. On the side walls are two ceremonial portraits, *Louis XV* and *Marie Leszczinska*, both painted by Carle Van Loo.

Carle Van Loo, *Marie Leszczinska, Queen of France*, 1747.

The Mercury Drawing Room

The Mercury and Apollo Drawing Rooms were the most luxurious in the Château of Versailles, in which was kept some of the famous silver furniture until it was melted down in 1689. In 1682, when Court and Government were officially established at Versailles, the Mercury Drawing Room was the State Bedchamber. For this original function, we have installed the bed commissioned by Louis-Philippe for the bedchamber of Louis XIV when Versailles was turned into a museum. It is also worth noting the presence to the right of the bed of *David playing the harp* by Le Dominiquin, one of Louis XIV's favourite paintings. The central motif of the ceiling painted by Jean-Baptiste de Champaigne shows *Mercury on his Chariot Drawn by Two Cocks*. The same artist painted the ceiling-coves representing *Alexander the Great and Ptolemy II surrounded by scholars and philosophers*. The automaton clock, which was a gift to Louis XIV from the clock-maker Antoine Morand in 1706, was undoubtedly only placed here in mid-18th century. When the hour strikes, the figures of Louis XIV and of Fame appear descending from a cloud.

Jean-Baptiste de Champaigne, *Mercury on his chariot drawn by two cocks* (detail), 1672-1681.

The Apollo Drawing Room

Versailles was the first royal château to have a throne room. The silver throne, standing as high as eight foot, was melted down in 1689, and was replaced much later, under Louis XV, by a gilt wood throne. A platform and the eyebolts in the arch mouldings show where the throne and its dais once stood. The Apollo Drawing Room was used for formal audiences. On the ceiling, Charles de La Fosse painted the Sun Chariot. The famous portrait of Louis XIV by Rigaud (see p. 6) hung in this room until the Revolution. The portrait of the reigning sovereign was hung opposite, *Louis XVI* by Antoine François Calet.

General view of the ceiling in the Apollo Room with, in the centre, the painting of Charles de La Fosse, *Apollon sur son char tiré par quatre chevaux et accompagné des Saisons,* (Apollo in his chariot pulled by four horses and accompanied by the seasons) 1672-1681.

The Grand Gallery

The War Drawing Room, the Hall of Mirrors and the Peace Drawing Room form an ensemble whose decor is devoted to the military victories and political successes of Louis XIV. This ensemble is not contemporary with the first major works carried out by the architect Le Vau. In the plan for a stone envelope around Louis XIII's little château, which he presented in 1668, the latter left a terrace on the west façade overlooking the gardens. It was Jules Hardouin-Mansart who on September 26, 1678 (the year of the Peace of Nijmegen) presented the King with plans for the construction of the present Hall of Mirrors. Work began immediately and was completed in 1686.

The War Drawing Room

The War Drawing Room evokes Louis XIV's victories over the allied powers during the war with Holland, and the Peace of Nijmegen which brought it to an end in 1678. The chimney-piece, designed by Le Brun, is decorated with bas-reliefs by Antoine Coysevox. The large medallion portrays an important episode in the war with Holland: Louis XIV is represented on horseback in classical dress on the occasion of the French troops' crossing of the Rhine on June 12, 1672. On the fireplace we can see Clio, the Muse of History, writing the history of the King. In collaboration with Le Conte, Arcy and Prou, Coysevox executed the trophies which surmount the mirrored false doors, reflecting the same spirit as the bas-reliefs of the fireplace.

The Hall of Mirrors

Detail of a mascaron adorning the vaulted ceiling in the Hall of Mirrors

Louis XIV initially had the Hall of Mirrors furnished with pieces in solid silver designed by Charles Le Brun. However, these were melted down in 1689 to meet the expenses of war. These original fittings were candelabra, pedestal tables, and tables for torches, and great vases to hold orange trees, all deftly worked by the finest silversmiths of the time. Under the Ancien Régime, the Hall of Mirrors functioned as a passageway giving access to the King's Apartment. Here gathered the courtiers who hoped to see the monarch on his way to the Chapel. Some took the opportunity to present a request. When he received extraordinary embassies, such as that of Siam in 1686, Louis XIV would have the silver throne moved here from its usual place in the Apollo Drawing Room. Grand celebrations were also held here, such as full-dress balls, or the masked balls given on the occasion of princely marriages.

In his ceiling-painting, Charles Le Brun portrayed the history of Louis XIV's reign, and its central theme is the war against Holland and its allies (1672-1678) and the War of Devolution (1667-1668). The whole composition is organised around a central motif entitled *The King governing alone*, in which one sees Louis XIV, face to face with the great European powers, turn away from his games and pleasures to contemplate the crown of immortality held out to him by Glory, and which is pointed out to him by Mars, the god of war. The candelabra were replaced in 1770 on the occasion of the marriage of the then future Louis XVI with the Archiduchesse Marie-Antoinette de Lorraine-Autriche. These are the candelabra which were reconstructed by moulding the six original preserved models, kept in the Apollo Drawing Room. This is the same for the twenty-four chandeliers which used to be hung only during evening celebrations.

The King governing alone and *The prosperous neighbouring powers of France*, 1681-1686.

The Peace Drawing Room

As its name suggests, the decoration of this drawing room is dedicated to peace: the peace which followed the wars represented in the War Drawing Room and the Hall of Mirrors, and that established by the Kings of France as an expression of France's dominant place in Europe. Above the fireplace is a painting by François Lemoyne (1729), showing *Louis XV offering Europe an olive branch*. This Drawing room was soon connected to the Queen's Apartment, to be used as the Games Room. It was thus separated from the Hall of Mirrors by a moving partition which closed off the connecting archway. Here, every Sunday, under the reign of Louis XV, the Queen Maria Leszczinska gave concerts of sacred and secular music which played an important role in the musical life of Versailles.

The King's Apartment

This part of the Château can be accessed from the Œil-de-Bœuf antechamber adjoining the Hall of Mirrors which allows visitors to view the Kings Guards Room and the antechamber of the Grand Couvert, without entering them. The visit continues via the King's Bedchamber. On the death of his wife in 1683, Louis XIV turned her interior apartments into the King's Apartment. These rooms were never returned to the Queen, which meant that, unlike the King, she actually had to live in her State Apartment.

The Guardroom and the Antechamber of the Grand Couvert

The Guardroom is decorated exclusively with white panelling; above the fireplace is Parrocel's painting of the *Battle of Leuze*, a tribute to the sentries recognisable in their blue coats. More richly decorated than the Guardroom, the First Antechamber was used every evening, under Louis XIV, for the Grand Couvert, that is, the meal that the King took in public. The King's table stood before the fireplace, his spoon, his knife and his fork were brought in a box wrought of gold called the Cadenas, hence the expression "mettre le couvert" or "to lay the table". The food was paraded with great pomp from the Grand Commun. Every Monday morning in the First Antechamber, a table was set out covered with a green velvet cloth, behind which the King was symbolically represented by an empty armchair: here courtiers could table their petitions, which were never left unanswered.

The Antechamber of the Œil-de-Bœuf

The Second Antechamber, known as the Œil-de-Bœuf due to the shape of the window in the cornice of the room, was only enlarged to its present size in 1701. It served as a "waiting room" for the ceremonies of the Lever and the Coucher, when the King rose or retired. The paintings by Bassan were replaced by different portraits of the royal family during the reign of Louis XIV, with, in particular, a large mythological composition by Jean Nocret.

Jean Nocret, *The family of Louis XIV in 1670, dressed up as mythological figures*, 1670.

The King's Bedchamber

This central room was originally the State Drawing Room. After the death of Queen Maria-Theresa, it was attached to the King's apartment and became generally known as "the room in which the King dresses". At that time, three archways opened onto the Hall of Mirrors for which the room acted as a sort of complement. In 1701, Louis XIV decided to turn the room into his bedchamber. It was here that the Sun King would die on September 1, 1715. After him, both Louis XV and Louis XVI would continue to use it for the ceremonies of the Lever and the Coucher. It was on the balcony, on October 6, 1789, that Louis XVI, the Queen and the Dauphin appeared before the crowd as the royal family was forced to leave Versailles for Paris. In 1701, when the State Drawing Room became the bedchamber, the archways opening onto the Hall of Mirrors were closed off and replaced by an alcove hung with velvet in the winter to match the furnishings, and brocade in the summer (embroidered with gold thread). It is the summer furnishings that were restored. At the same time, Coustou carved the relief depicting *France watching over the sleeping King*, which dominates the King's bed. Among the paintings embedded in the panelling and which still remain in place, two in particular typify the interests of Louis XIV: *Self-portrait* by Van Dyck and *Caesar's Denarius* by Valentin de Boulogne.

Anton Van Dyck, *Self-portrait*, 17th century.

The Council Chamber

The King's armchair.

The former State Cabinet of Louis XIV and the King's Wig Cabinet were joined together in 1755 to form the present Council Chamber where one can observe in the panelling, carved by Rousseau to designs by Gabriel, medallions evoking the work of the King. The Council of State met here on Sundays and Wednesdays, and occasionally on Mondays, while the Council of Finances met on Tuesdays and Saturdays. Once or twice a month there would be Extraordinary Councils, such as the Council of Despatches. The King would be seated in an armchair and the ministers on folding chairs. Also, during the reign of Louis XIV and his successors, the King would summon his family here for certain ceremonies, such as the signing of the registers during princely marriages. It was also here that, in 1700, Louis XIV accepted the Spanish crown for his grandson the Duke of Anjou from whom Juan Carlos, the current King of Spain, descends.

The Queen's State Apartment

The characteristic symmetry which marks Versailles existed from the beginning between the Queen's Apartment and the King's. Both had the same number of rooms, the decoration of the ceilings was devoted to the same deities and planets, and they differed only in the paintings of the ceiling-coves, which in the King's Apartment portrayed male, and in the Queen's, female figures.

The Queen's Bedchamber

It was in this room, in public, that the Queen gave birth to the heirs to the throne. In her *Memoirs*, Madame Campan, who was Marie-Antoinette's First Woman of the Bedchamber, described what such a birth could be like: "the moment that Vermond the accoucheur announced 'The Queen is about to give birth', the crowds of spectators who rushed into her room were so numerous and disorderly that one thought the Queen would perish... Two Savoyards got up on the furniture the more easily to see the Queen, who was facing the fireplace on a bed got ready for her labour."

View of the fireplace featuring a bust created in 1783 by Félix Lecomte.

The Peers' Salon

In the Peers' Salon, the Queen of France held official audiences, and ladies newly admitted to Court were presented to her. Certain elements of the décor, the ceiling in particular, which portrays an allegory of Mercury, recall the fact that originally the Queen's Apartment was symmetrical with the King's. The furniture is that designed for Marie-Antoinette in 1785.

The Antechamber of the Grand Couvert

In Queen Maria-Theresa's day, this room was the Room of the Queen's Guard, hence the ceiling decorated with warlike themes. Visitors who had obtained an audience with the Queen would have to wait here before entering the Peers' Salon or the Bedchamber. This room was also used for concerts and theatrical performances. The name Grand Couvert comes from that of the ceremonial requiring that the King and Queen eat certain meals in public. One of the most noteworthy was the meal that Louis XV and Maria Leszczinska took here in the company of the young Mozart on January 1, 1764. Out of the paintings hung in the Antechamber of the Grand Couvert, the most famous is the large painting by

Élisabeth Vigée-Lebrun exhibited in the 1787 Drawing Room. The painting depicts Marie-Antoinette with her three children: Madame Royale who survived the Revolution; the Duke of Normandy, future Louis XVII, who died in the Prison du Temple in 1795; and the Dauphin, who died in 1789, pointing to an empty cradle which should have held Madame Sophie, who died at a very young age before the painting was completed.

Élisabeth Vigée-Lebrun, *Marie-Antoinette of Lorraine-Habsbourg, Queen of France, and her children*, 1789.

The Guardroom

In the corners of the ceiling, Noël Coypel painted the figures of courtiers leaning over into the room, watching the comings and goings. This room, set aside for the use of the Queen's guards, was constantly cluttered with screens hiding campbeds, tables and racks for their arms. It was here that on the morning of October 6, 1789, guards lost their lives helping the Queen seek refuge by the King's side.

The Marble Staircase

Noël Coypel, *Northeast spandrel of the ceiling in the Guardroom representing courtiers* (detail), around 1781.

This feature was also called the Queen's Staircase because it originally served only Queen Maria-Theresa's Apartment. In 1681, it replaced a more modest staircase and, after the death of the Queen in 1683, was used to reach Louis XIV's new apartment. It was designed as a worthy match for the Ambassadors' Staircase. In addition to the marble décor and the gilt lead sculpture by Massou symbolising the marriage of Louis XIV and Maria-Theresa, the Marble Staircase is adorned with a vast painting showing a palace perspective, the architecture of which was painted by Meusnier, the people by Poerson and the flowers by Belin de Fontenay.

The History Galleries

After the Queen's State Apartment, the visit continues via the history galleries created under the reign of Louis-Philippe in the 19th century: the Coronation Room, the 1792 Room, the Hall of Battles and the 1830 Room. Other parts belonging to the history galleries can be discovered during guided tours (see p. 62-63).

Jacques Louis David, *Coronation of Emperor Napoleon I and coronation of Josephine at Notre-Dame de Paris, 2 December 1804*, 1808.

The Coronation Room

This room was originally the site of the Château's third chapel. When in 1682 the Court and Government were officially established at Versailles, it served as the common guardroom of the King's and Queen's guards. Permanently cluttered with the sedan chairs of the ladies of the court, benches, screens and arms racks, and hung with painted canvas, courtiers nicknamed this room the "magasin" or storeroom. Here every Maundy Thursday, the King would wash the feet of thirteen poor children. Its present appearance and name date from the reign of Louis-Philippe who installed the painting by David, depicting the *Coronation of Emperor Napoleon I and coronation of Josephine at Notre-Dame de Paris, 2 December 1804*.

The Hall of Battles

Situated in the South Wing (or Princes' Wing), covering the first floor and the attic on the park side, the Hall of Battles took the place of the apartments reserved for the members of the royal family. The architects Nepveu and Fontaine designed the Hall of Battles as a setting for the vast paintings dedicated to the great French victories, from Tolbiac, won by Clovis in 497, to Wagram, a victory for Napoleon in 1809. It was Louis-Philippe's express desire for the busts of the great officers and princes of royal blood who died for France to be exhibited in the Hall of Battles, along with the commemorative plaques bearing their names and dates. A complement to the Hall of Mirrors, it leads to the 1830 room, created to honour Louis-Philippe's accession to the throne and the new constitutional monarchy born out of the 1830 Revolution. The paintings forming the décor of the Hall of Battles are not of equal quality: *Marignan* by Évariste Fragonard, *The Entry of Henry IV into Paris* and *The Battle of Austerlitz* by Gérard are striking. However, Delacroix's *Saint Louis in Taillebourg* is particularly famous for the artist's skill in creating an ardent and romantic image of an event that had taken place over six hundred years previously.

The Apartments of the Dauphin and Dauphine

The visit to the State Apartments ends on the ground floor with the Dauphin's and Dauphine's apartments. From the late 17th century onwards, as heirs to the throne, the Dauphin and Dauphine each enjoyed access to an adjoining apartment on the ground floor spread out to the southwest of the Château's main part. Visitors can discover the rooms at their leisure via the ground-floor access point at the bottom of the Queen's Staircase. A small staircase, its present appearance dating from the reign of Louis XVI, leads down to the Antechamber of the Œil-de-Boeuf in the Dauphin's Apartment, the library of which communicates with the Dauphine's Apartment. They aim to depict the surroundings in which the Dauphin, son of Louis XV, father of Louis XVI, lived with his wife Maria-Josepha of Saxony. Despite the changes made by Louis-Philippe, some of the rooms retain all or part of their panelling, namely the Dauphin's bedchamber, his State Cabinet and Library, together with the Dauphine's Private Cabinet. It should not be

View of the Dauphine's bedchamber.

forgotten that, during the 17th century, the Grand Dauphin, son of Louis XIV, turned it into an apartment renowned for its beauty and lavish collections, which, during the infancy of Louis XV, was to become the abode of the Regent Philippe d'Orléans. Although it has not been possible to retrieve all of the furnishings which adorned these apartments, at least certain objects were found: the globe commissioned in 1781 by Louis XIV from the geographer Mancelle, for the education of his son; the desk by Bernard Van Risen Burgh and Œben, delivered for the Dauphin in 1756, and constantly used by Louis XVI in his library under the eaves, in then his Privy Purse Cabinet; or the bureau delivered in 1745 by Bernard Van Risen Burgh for the first Dauphine and reused by the Dauphine of Saxony; and the commode by Gaudreaux, delivered for the Dauphine's bedchamber at Fontainebleau.

View of the library
and the Dauphin's bedchamber.

Other tours

I n addition to the large public spaces and so as to gain a better understanding of court life, it is possible to visit several confidential parts of the Château with a guide such as the private apartments of the King and Queen, the Mesdames' Apartment (Louis XV's daughters), the Opera Royal and the continuation of Louis-Philippe's history galleries.

The King's Small Apartment

Previous double page
View of Louis XVI's Library.

Named the King's Private Apartment during the reign of Louis XIV, this suite was known as the Interior Apartment under Louis XV and Louis XVI. After having been reserved solely for the Sovereign's collections during the reign of the Great King, it became a proper apartment in 1737, where Louis XV then Louis XVI actually lived.

Louis XV's Bedchamber

When, in 1738, Louis XV decided to install a bedchamber smaller than that of Louis XIV, he still continued to use his grandfather's bedchamber for the ceremonies of the Lever and the Coucher. It was in here that he died of smallpox on May 10, 1774. It was also here that Louis XVI spent his last night at Versailles, from the 5th to the 6th of October 1789.

Armand Vincent de Montpetit,
Portrait of Louis XV, 1774.

The Clock Cabinet

Constituting two rooms, the second of which led through an archway into the next, and forming the cabinets in which Louis XIV exhibited some of his paintings, the Clock Cabinet underwent several transformations under Louis XV before acquiring its definitive appearance in 1760, in order to set off the astronomical clock designed by Passamant, kept in this room from 1754. Delamaire's barometer, commissioned by Louis XV, delivered during the reign of Louis XVI and only installed under Charles X in 1827, stands opposite. The complex mechanism of the astronomical clock enables it to tell the time, the day of the week, the date in the month, the month, the year and the phase of the moon until 9999. Inside the crystal globe above one can see the planets revolving around the sun according to Copernican principles. Nothing short of a technical marvel, the entire mechanism is activated by the movement of a single pendulum.

The Private Cabinet

Having been transformed several times, the Work Cabinet or Private Cabinet acquired its definitive décor in 1760. The magnificent panelling both here and in the Clock Cabinet had been previously carved by Verbeckt and still remains today. The large roll-top desk commissioned from Œben and Riesener dates from the reign of Louis XV (1759-1769).

Louis XVI's Library

Like the previous room, known as the Golden Dinner ware Room d'Or, and the following, known as the Porcelain Dining Room, the Library is on the site of the old Ambassadors' Staircase and the Petite Galerie. It was created on Louis XVI's accession to the throne, in 1774. Of its original furniture, in addition to the globes representing the earth and the planets, the table still remains, the top being made from a single piece measuring 2.10 metres in diameter.

The Porcelain Dining Room

This room reached its present size in 1769 when Louis XV joined his daughter Madame Adélaïde's Apartment to his private cabinets. However, the furniture and fabric are those designed in 1785 for Louis XVI. The different porcelain pieces all originate from royal services. They serve as a reminder that every year, towards Christmas, the King would exhibit in this room the latest Sèvres porcelain. Everyone could admire and buy them. The walls are hung with Sèvres porcelain plaques painted after Oudry's tapestries depicting the royal hunts of Louis XV and transposed here to represent the hunts of Louis XVI in the forests of Compiègne and Fontainebleau. These plaques were already part of the décor under the Ancien Régime.

Louis XVI's Games Room

During the reign of Louis XIV, this was the Cabinet of Curios and Rare Objects, where were exhibited some of the most precious items from the royal collections. Madame Adélaïde's antechamber in 1753, the Cabinet of Curios and Rare Objects was completely transformed in 1769 for Louis XV who wanted to turn it into a library, Louis XVI chose to install his Games Room here instead. It was for this purpose that the chairs designed by Boulard were commissioned in 1785, and have now returned to their proper place. The corner cupboards delivered by Riesener in 1775 and the paintings by Van Blarenberghe also originated in this room. The latter were gouaches commissioned by Louis XVI to commemorate the different victories of his grandfather Louis XV.

The King's Private Cabinets

The King's Private Cabinets is the name given to a suite of rooms above the King's Private Apartment, which was the private domain of Louis XV and Louis XVI. The library and its annexes, and the Geography and Physics Cabinets illustrate the kings' interest in scholarship and research. Some rooms also became apartments for the King's intimates.

Madame Du Barry's Library

Created in 1753 for Madame Adélaïde when the princess lived in the present new rooms, it acquired its definitive appearance in 1769, when it was joined to Madame Du Barry's Apartment which occupied part of the King's Private Cabinets.

The King's Staircase

This staircase led to both the King's Private Apartment and Private Cabinets. It was the scene of the attempt on the life of Louis XV on January 5, 1757, by Damiens, as the King was getting ready to leave for Trianon.

Marie-Antoinette's Small Apartments

View of the Billiard Room.

Now reduced to just a few rooms (oratory, bathroom), the Queen's Private Cabinets were at their largest in the time of Marie-Antoinette. The Queen had use of not only Maria Leszczinska's private cabinets on the first floor, but also a suite of small rooms located on the second floor, around the inner courtyards, and a proper apartment on the ground floor where Madame Sophie, Aunt of Louis XVI, had lived until her death in 1782. In her *Memoirs*, Madame Campan, Marie-Antoinette's First Woman of the Bedchamber, states that "The list of people received in the Queen's private rooms had been given to the Ushers of the Bedchamber by the Princess de Lamballe, and the people listed there could avail themselves of this favour only on days when the Queen desired the company of her intimates... Persons of the first rank at Court would sometimes ask her for private audiences."

The Queen's Private Cabinet

This replaced the night apartment of the Duke of Bourgogne, father of Louis XV, and Maria Leszczinska's private cabinet, and was granted to Marie-Antoinette who received her favourite artists, the painter, Madame Vigée-Lebrun, the composer Gluck, her old musicteacher, and Mlle Bertin, her dressmaker.

Jean-Baptiste André Gautier d'Agoty,
*Marie-Antoinette playing the harp in her
bedchamber at Versailles*, 18th century.

The Meridian Cabinet

After having once been Maria Leszczinska's private drawing room, a staircase was built here in 1770, connecting the Dauphin's Apartment, the future Louis XVI, to that of his wife Marie-Antoinette, who already occupied the Queen's Apartment. The present drawing room was fitted out in 1781 on the birth of the first Dauphin. The décor of the panelling (opposite) serves as a reminder of the event, as do the carvings on the console.

Mesdames' Apartments

The only remaining apartments belonging to the daughters of Louis XV are those occupied by Madame Adélaïde and Madame Victoire from 1769 until the Revolution. These apartments replaced Louis XIV's former Bath Apartment, altered to make apartments for Madame de Pompadour and the Comtesse de Toulouse. According to Madame Campan, "Louis XV went down to Madame Adélaïde's apartment each morning by a hidden staircase. He often brought and drank coffee that he had made himself. Madame Adélaïde would tug at a bell-pull, which would warn Madame Victoire of the King's visit..."

Jean-Marc Nattier, *Madame Victoire of France*, around 1747, and *Madame Adélaïde of France*, 1756.

View of the Apartment of Madame Victoire.

The Opera

Louis XIV commissioned the first plans for the Royal Opera from Mansart and Vigarani in 1682; however, war and financial difficulties towards the end of his reign meant that it could not be built. The second design, for the same location at the end of the North Wing, was presented by Gabriel to Louis XV in 1748, but it too remained unbuilt. It was only after the marriage of the Dauphin, the future Louis XVI, to the Archiduchesse Marie-Antoinette, that the work was carried out and the opera finally completed and inaugurated on May 16, 1770. The opera house is in the shape of a truncated ellipse. It was entirely built of wood for reasons of economy and rapidity, which provides excellent acoustics. Its imitation marble décor is embelished with sculptures by Pajou, and the ceiling painted by Durameau represents the triumph of Apollo, god of the arts. The architect Gabriel and the engineer Arnoult had planned a mechanism which would raise the floor of the auditorium to the same level as the stage, decorated to match the rest of the room. The theatre would then be able to host full-dress balls, dances where the ladies wore jewellery, tiaras and formal dress.

The History Galleries

Alongside the history galleries accessible during the visit of the State Apartments (see p. 44-45), other parts are gradually revealed during guided tours.

The Crusades Galleries

The ceilings of the five Crusades Galleries are adorned with the coats of arms of the families who, in the Middle Ages, went to free the Holy Places. The most famous of the many paintings, all of which were retrospectives, was *The Entry of the Crusaders into Constantinople* by Delacroix (the original is now in the Louvre has been replaced by a copy). This décor was to serve as a setting for the door of the Knights Hospital of the Holy Sepulchre in Rhodes, a gift to Louis-Philippe from the Ottoman Sultan.

The 19th-century Rooms

Antoine Jean Gros, *General Bonaparte at the Pont d'Arcole, on Novembre 17, 1796*, 1798.

Léon Bonnat, *Portrait of Victor Hugo*, 1879.

In his desire to reconcile the different regimes, Louis-Philippe decided not to favour a particular period of French history. He thus devoted the whole of the ground floor of the South Wing to the Empire, to which should be added the second-floor rooms, above the Queen's Apartment and the South Wing, running alongside the vault of the Hall of Battles. Among the works devoted to this short but turbulent period of French history, stretching from the Revolution to the end of the Empire, the portrait of *General Bonaparte at the Pont d'Arcole on November 17, 1796*, by Gros, is surely one of the most magnificent. Great writers also have their place in the history galleries. Note the celebrated portraits of Victor Hugo by Bonnat and Chateaubriand by Girodet.

The Gardens

Like the Château, the gardens are a museum in their own right. Louis XIV designed them to be considered as such. Subordinate yet complementary to the Château, the grounds represent the apotheosis of gardens "à la française" with countless stunning features achieved by long perspectives, regular outlines, parterres, groves and stretches of water reflecting the buildings.

West Side

Beyond the Château, to the west, stretch the gardens and the park, laid out around a main east-west axis, perpendicular to the Château, and a secondary axis from north to south, running alongside the façades.

View of one of the
Water Parterres pools

The Water Parterre

At the foot of the buildings, Le Nôtre created the parterres, designed to be viewed from the terraces. They were also intended to set off the Château's architecture. The two perfectly horizontal ponds of the Water Parterre, mirrors reflecting the façades, created later (around 1685), demonstrate this concept pushed to the extreme. Statues of stone, marble, lead and bronze populate the gardens with people and animals, often derived from mythology or allegories. Le Nôtre made sure that the sculptures emphasised rather than interfered with the lines of the garden. Thus, several powerful recumbent figures came to adorn the edges of the Water Parterre. These bronze masterpieces depict the rivers of France, symbols of the kingdom.

The Grand Perspective

Openness and scope characterise the work of Le Nôtre. Before him, the gardens were closed and relatively modest in size. They now open onto the surrounding countryside and have changed scale. Le Nôtre also gives greater importance to the central axis, around which all of the other parts of the garden have been arranged. Starting from the terrace of the Château, the Grand Perspective draws the eye to the horizon. As it moves further away, it crosses the parterres, descends through the groves, follows the canal between the forests of the park, gently rising through the countryside towards the sky. Thus making its way from a strongly architectural to a more natural setting, the axial route starts with a simple pathway between the ponds of the Water Parterre, goes down the steps, and skirts round the Fountain of Latona. After a small slope and another pathway between the Latona Parterres, it passes through the long grassy stretch of the Royal Avenue or *Green Carpet*, bordered on either side with greenery, and opens onto the Fountain of Apollo and its vast esplanade, before merging with the Grand Canal 1,800 meters in length.

The Latona fountain

Inspired by Ovid's *The Metamorphoses*, the Latona Fountain illustrates the legend of Apollo and Diana's mother protecting her children against the insults of Lycian peasants, and asking Jupiter to avenge her, which he does by turning them into frogs and lizards.

The central marble sculpture by the Marsy brothers, representing Latona and her children, was originally built on a rock in 1670. It was surrounded by six frogs half-emerging from the water, and twenty four other frogs placed outside the fountain, on the grass platform. Originally, the goddess faced the palace. This arrangement was changed by Jules Hardouin-Mansart between 1687 and 1689. The rock was replaced by a marble pyramid and Latona now faces the Grand Canal. The Latona Fountain is extended by a parterre on which you find the two ponds of Lizards.

Gaspard and Balthasar Marsy,
Latone et ses enfants (Latona and
her children), 1668-1671.

The Fountain of Apollo

Jean-Baptiste Tuby, *Apollo on his chariot*, 1668-1670.

This vast pond owes its décor, which deals with the major theme of the mythological, symbolical and political concepts developed throughout the gardens, to its prime position. Just as Louis XIV is identified with the sun god, Phoebus Apollo, similarly, Apollo rising above the waves denotes the rising of the sun and the dawning of a promising reign. Le Brun, who designed the sculptures, expanded on the theme: he shows the god in his chariot drawn by four horses, surrounded by four Tritons and four sea monsters. He entrusted the execution of the sculpture to one of the most talented sculptors, Jean-Baptiste Tuby, a Roman in the King's service. Like all of the exceptional royal commissions, the Apollo sculpture was executed at the Gobelins works. Cast between 1668 and 1670, it was gilded after its installation.

North Side

A natural slope leads from the Water Parterre to the Fountain of Neptune enabling multiple water effects. The same central aisle principle is used here, opening up the view and lined with groves surrounded by arbours, which characterise the east-west axis. The Grotto of Thetis was nearby until 1684. Its water features and stunning interior already used to attract many visitors at the time.

The North Parterre

Planted out with box trees and grass, brightened up with a few flowers and dotted with trimmed yew trees (topiaries), the North Parterre embraces the incline of the North Wing. The décor of the fountains of the North Parterre matches the sculptures of marine deities adorning the façades of the North Wing. It also serves as a reminder of the closeness of two elements that have now disappeared: Louis XIV's Bath Apartment and the Grotto of Thetis. Tritons, Sirens, dolphins and crayfish populate the Pyramid Fountain and the two Crown ponds.

François Girardon, *The Pyramid*, 1672.

The Dragon Fountain and the Fountain of Neptune

Dominated by two large open-air pools, the Water Avenue, leading to the Dragon Fountain, separates two groves currently undergoing restoration. It is also called the Allée des Marmousets since it is lined with twenty-two bronze sculptures of children (after Le Brun's designs). These figures alternate with topiaries grown in the unusual shapes in which Louis XIV's gardeners used to trim the yew trees. In the Dragon Fountain (one of the oldest in Versailles), the water theme merges with the legend of Apollo, since the dragon in actual fact symbolises Python, the mythical serpent that Apollo slew with his bow and arrow. The water jet shooting out of the dragon's mouth, reaching up to 27 metres, is the highest of all of the fountains. Below the Dragon Fountain, the immense Fountain of Neptune comprises 58 jets and 147 hydraulic effects. Depending on the shape of the pipe outlets, the water shoots out in bubbles, waves, streams or showers. Laid out by Le Nôtre, the Fountain of Neptune's only decoration initially consisted in the large lead vases embellishing the parapet. Sixty years later, continuing the work of his great grandfather, Louis XV added monumental statues, also made from lead, representing Neptune and Amphitrite, Ocean and Proteus. Beyond the fountain, a densely wooded area closes off the park, protecting it from the north wind.

View of the Water Avenue with a group of interlaced children in bronze in the foreground.

South Side

Instead of natural slopes on this side, there is a series of three terraces: on the same level as the Château is the South Parterre, the end of which drops vertically onto the Orangery; further along and lower down is the Pond of the Swiss, the exaggerated length of which was calculated to enhance the perspective.

The South Parterre

Its arrangement of box trees interspersed with flowers is landscaped in arabesques beneath the windows of the Queen's Apartment on the first floor of the Château. Previously named the Parterre of Flowers or Parterre of Love, it is located above the Orangery. It can be reached via a porch surrounded by the oldest sculptures in the grounds, *Cupids on a sphinx*. The bronze children, modelled by Sarazin and smelted by Duval in 1668, were placed on marble sphinxes sculpted by Lerambert.

Nicolas Duval, Jacques Houzeau and Louis Lerambert, after a model by Jacques Sarazin, *Cupid on a sphinx*, 1667-1668.

The Orangerie
and the Pond of Swiss

The Orangery is tucked away underground below the Château. Flanked with the great 100-step stairway, it ensures the stability of the grounds. Through its vast space (main gallery 155 metres long and 13 meters high), simple lines and beautiful arches, the Orangery is one of the places in which Jules Hardouin-Mansart most successfully displayed his talents as a great architect. Its south-facing position and doubleglazing stabilise the temperature at between 5 and 8°C in winter. It houses 1,080 delicate trees, all of which are planted in boxes: orange trees from Portugal and Italy, lemon trees and pomegranate trees (some of which are over 200 years old), oleanders, and palm trees (since the turn of the century). The trees produce little fruit since they are pruned into a decorative spherical form. The gardeners bring them out in mid-May and take them back inside in mid-October. In the distance lies the vast expanse of the Pond of the Swiss, the name of which refers to the contribution of the reinforcement regiments called in to drain the marshes and dig the pond. This was at the time when there were tens of thousand of men working at Versailles.

The Avenues
and Groves

Away from the central avenue, the surrounding wooded areas are waiting to be discovered, criss-crossed with a regular network of avenues. The wider, longer avenues, providing distant views, intersect at right angles. Other pathways, curved and diagonal, shorter and more narrow, lead to the groves (eight in the north and six in the south). From the large avenues, only walls of foliage can be seen. In the reign of Louis XIV, these walls of trees were espaliered at a great height and the foliage of the trees fixed to the frames was not allowed to grow over 15 metres. The strictly cubic appearance of these wooded areas reflected the desire of the King and his gardener to create a veritable architectural structure of foliage. In contrast to the rigid appearance of the outside, fantasy reigned within, surprising visitors with varied water effects in the midst of clearings in which the rockwork, trellis-work or architectural décor was enhanced by numerous sculptures. From the 17th century, a number of regulations intervened concerning access to the groves, sometimes accessible to all, sometimes strictly limited. They can now be seen through their railings, or better still, entered during guided tours or during the Grandes-Eaux, when the fountains play at Versailles. Since their creation, some of the groves have been subjected to alterations. Among these, the renowned Maze Grove was decorated with 39 fountains illustrating the *Fables* of La Fontaine, and then sadly replaced by the Queen's Grove in the time of Marie-Antoinette.

View of the Autumn Avenue with the Bacchus or Autumn Fountain.

The Fountains
of the Seasons

Two major avenues, running parallel to the
Grand Perspective, cut through the walls of
foliage concealing the groves. These are bordered with lines of trees, rigorously pruned
both in height and thickness, forming smaller
avenues on either side. These are the Avenues
of the Four Seasons. The Bacchus Fountain
decorates one of the four ponds placed at
the intersection in the Avenues of the Four
Seasons: Bacchus or Autumn, Saturn or Winter,
Flora or Spring, Ceres or Summer. They served
as a reminder that the sun god determined not
only the course of the day, but also the course
of the year.

François Girardon, *Saturn*, 1672-1678.

Gaspard and Balthasar Marsy, *Bacchus*, 1672-1678.

The Ballroom
and the Colonnade Grove

The Ballroom (or Bosquet des Rocailles) and the Colonnade groves have been preserved as they were in the reign of Louis XIV. Almost contemporary with each other (both were created between 1680 and 1690), they are, nonetheless, very different since one was designed by a gardener, André Le Nôtre, and the other, by an architect, Jules Hardouin-Mansart. One makes use of natural elements: streams of water, rockwork and shells, vegetation covering the embankments and terraces. The other, a cold, formal peristyle of 32 columns surrounding Girardon's masterpiece, *Pluto abducting Proserpine*, is purely architecture and sculpture, marble and water. When Louis XIV asked Le Nôtre his opinion on the Colonnade, the gardener replied, "Sire, you turned a stonemason into a gardener, he has played you one of his tricks". Louis XIV thought so highly of his gardens that he wrote *The Manner of Presenting the Gardens of Versailles* and had them painted by several artists. This gouache by Cotelle shows that the centre of the Ballroom was originally occupied by an island reached by small bridges. The Court could there be entertained by dinners, light refreshments, ballets or musical interludes, as in the other groves.

Opposite
François Girardon, *Pluto abducting Proserpine*, 1675-1695.

Below
View of the Ballroom or Bosquet des Rocailles

The Dome and Enceladus Grove

These two groves, adjacent to the fountain of Apollo, illustrate two trends in French art at the time of Louis XIV. The serenity of the Dome Grove (above) contrasts with the cruel, dramatic effect of the fountain of Enceladus (opposite), created by Marsy in 1675-1677 based on a design by Charles Le Brun. Enceladus, leader of the giants, rebelled against Jupiter. In order to attack Mount Olympus, he piled mountain upon mountain. However, struck down by Jupiter, he disappeared, crushed under the rocks, uttering a final curse symbolised by the powerful jet shooting out of his mouth. The Fountain of Enceladus had considerably deteriorated since the 17th century. It has recently been fully restored to how it was in approximately 1700, a time when, having reached maturity, the gardens of Versailles were in a state of perfection. The trelliswork supporting sweet-scented plants was renewed, along with the small rockwork fountains, the entire hydraulic system and the triple turf-covered treads. The statue of the giant was also fully restored.

Gaspard Marsy, *Enceladus*, 1675-1676.

Fountain sculpture by Jean-Michel Othoniel, grove by Louis Benech, 2015

The Water Theatre Grove

Created between 1671 and 1674 by André Le Nôtre for the feasts of Louis XIV, the grove was designed as a leafy theatre with a raised part for the actors, and stands for the audience. It was composed of a multitude of fountains, the water effects of which played with the verdant architecture and trellises.

It was destroyed in 1775 under the reign of Louis XVI and gave way to an arrangement of paths and lawns. This new design is what has long inspired its name as the Bosquet du Rond Vert (the grove of the green circle).

In 2003, as part of a park replanting project, the boundary trees were renewed.

In 2015, a new Water Theatre was inaugurated thanks to landscaper Louis Benech and artist Jean-Michel Othoniel. Their contemporary creation has given new life to the grove: water features with arabesque fountains in ornate Murano glass, evoking Louis XIV's dance steps.

The Baths of Apollo Grove

The Baths of Apollo Grove, concealed by the surrounding greenery, is particularly striking due to its size and broken relief. It was created almost a century after the older groves. It was during the replanting of the park ordered by Louis XVI in 1775 that the painter Hubert Robert completely redesigned the existing grove in which the three remarkable sculptures were already found: *Apollo Served by Nymphs*, and the two lateral groups, *The Horses of the Sun, Groomed by the Tritons*. Louis XIV had originally commissioned these works for the Grotto of Thetis. This grotto, sheltered beneath a pool, was a cool, precious place, with a carpet of shells and mirrors, the marine dwelling of the nymph, and night-time refuge of Phoebus Apollo. It had to be destroyed during the construction of the North Wing. Hubert Robert takes up the idea of the grotto again, but treats it according to the 18th century liking for wild nature with rocks and waterfalls. This group is the sculptural masterpiece of Versailles. It depicts the morning ablutions of the deity as he prepares for his daily task, after having rested at the nymph Thetis' abode. Composed of seven figures carved in white marble, it was executed by François Girardon, who carved the four main figures, and Thomas Regnaudin, who carved the three nymphs in the background. Girardon was Louis XIV's favourite sculptor. A great friend and close colleague of Le Brun and Le Nôtre, he appears in all the major sites. His masters were Classical Antiquity and Nature. Here, this fluid, majestic young god recaptures the features of the famous *Apollo Belvedere*. The delicate flesh tones, the flowing robes, and the precision of the engravings on the plates bear witness to the sensitivity and brilliance of the artist. Copies have replaced the originals which are in safe storage.

View of the three marble groups sculptures forming the Fountains of Apollo nestled in the Grotto with, to the left, the *Chevaux du Solei* (Horses of the Sun) by Gaspard and Balthasar Marsy, in the centre, *Apollon servi par les nymphes* (Apollo served by the nymphs) by François Girardon and Thomas Regnaudin and, to the right

The Trianon Châteaux and Marie-Antoinette's Estate

To the northwest of the Château, on the former site of the village of Trianon acquired by Louis XIV, stand the Châteaux of Grand Trianon and Petit Trianon. Built respectively by Louis XIV and Louis XV to escape the crowds and stifling etiquette of the palace, they are the perfect setting for a delightful walk enhanced by remarkable architectural and natural features.

The Grand Trianon

In 1668, Louis XIV bought a village named Trianon, which he joined to the Versailles estate and demolished. A pavilion decorated with blue and white tiles, which became known as the Porcelain Trianon, was built there in 1670. In 1687, the King decided to replace it with a larger building, the work of Mansart, which became known as the Marble Trianon from the way in which it was decorated. From then on until the fall of the Second Empire in 1870, the Trianon was constantly inhabited, apart from during the Revolution. However, it is mainly the installations commissioned by Napoleon I and Louis-Philippe that still remain in this dwelling, fully restored in 1965 by order of General de Gaulle.

Jean Cotelle the Younger, *View of the Grand Trianon from the parterres, with Flore and Zephyr*, 18th century.

The Napoleon's Bedchamber

Louis XV's Former State Cabinet, this room successively became the bedchamber of Napoleon, Princess Helene of Mecklenburg, wife of the Louis-Philippe's eldest son. Louis-Philippe often visited Trianon while work was being carried out to convert Versailles into a museum. The room has been restored to how it was in the time of Napoleon, with his fawn, purple and silver silks.

The Mirror Drawing Room

Strikingly decorated with mirrors, hence its name, this vast room in turn served as a state cabinet for the princes who inhabited the Left Wing of Trianon, Louis XIV himself, then his son the Grand Dauphin. After the Revolution, Madame, mother of Emperor Napoleon, Empress Marie-Louise and, lastly, Louis-Philippe lived there.

The Petit Trianon

Élisabeth Vigée-Lebrun, *Portrait of Queen Marie-Antoinette with rose*, 1783.

Between 1763 and 1768, Gabriel built a small square château, each façade of which was decorated differently, the richest being that with the tall Corinthian columns overlooking the French Garden. The interior panelling dates from the time of Louis XV, apart from in the Mechanical Mirror Room created for Marie-Antoinette. The Petit Trianon was in effect a gift to Marie-Antoinette from Louis XVI on his accession to the throne. The Queen then transformed the garden and had the rare plants transferred to the King's Garden in Paris (Jardin des Plantes). She asked the architect Mique and the painter Hubert Robert to design an English Garden in its place: hence the appearance of small brooks, picturesque views and lawns. The Château hosts what is certainly the most famous portrait of the Queen, *Marie-Antoinette with rose* painted by her favourite artist, Élisabeth Vigée-Lebrun. The sovereign is depicted creating a bouquet of roses, undoubtedly in her Trianon Garden.

View of the Queen's Bedchamber.

In 1777, Mique built the Rock Pavilion and the small mock-antique temple, known as the Temple of Love. In 1780, the small theatre was built, in which Marie-Antoinette deigned to appear and thus ensure the success of Beaumarchais' *Marriage of Figaro*.

The Queen's Hamlet

It was the Queen's Hamlet that made Marie-Antoinette's garden famous. Like Madame de Lamballe at Rambouillet and the Condés at Chantilly, Marie-Antoinette wanted a village of her own, whose houses, modelled on the style of Normandy cottages, would in fact be very elegant inside. Between 1783 and 1785, Mique built twelve houses, of which ten still stand, among them the Queen's Cottage, the Billiard Room, the Mill, the Boudoir, and the Pigeon Loft. Mique had designed a tower joined to the Dairy by a small gallery. It use to be possible to climb to the top via an outside staircase which no longer exists. From the top of the tower, one could fish with a line in the adjacent pond hence its name the Fishery Tower. However, it was more often called the Marlborough Tower (below), after the song made famous by the aptly named Madame Poitrine (bosom in French), the Dauphin's nurse.

Timeline

1623-1624: Louis XIII orders the construction of a hunting lodge on a hill in Versailles

1631: Louis XIII asks Philibert Le Roy to build a château on the site of the hunting lodge.

1643: Louis XIII stays at Versailles for the last time.

1660: Marriage of Louis XIV to Maria Theresa of Austria. On October 25, the King brings his wife to Versailles.

1664: Festivities of *Les Plaisirs de l'île enchantée*.

1668: *Grand Divertissement* at Versailles.

1682: Louis XIV declares Versailles the official residence of the court and seat of government.

1686: Completion of the Hall of Mirrors.

1710: Consecration of the chapel on June 5.

1715: September 1, death of Louis XIV. September 9, Louis XV abandons Versailles for Vincennes.

1722: Louis XV returns to live at Versailles.

1736: September 26, opening of the Hercules Salon.

1757: Attempt on Louis XV's life by Damiens.

1768: The Petit Trianon is completed.

1770: Opening of the Opera Royal on the occasion of the marriage of the future Louis XVI with Marie-Antoinette.

1774: May 10, Louis XV dies of smallpox at Versailles.

1777: Visit of Joseph II, Emperor of Austria, the Queen's brother.

1783: Signing of the Treaty of Versailles, acknowledging the independence of the United States of America.

1783-1786: Construction of the Queen's Hamlet.

1789: May 5, opening of the States General. October 6, the King, the royal family and the court leave Versailles for good after the Château is overrun.

1837: June 10, Louis-Philippe inaugurates the museum dedicated to the glories of France.

Genealogy

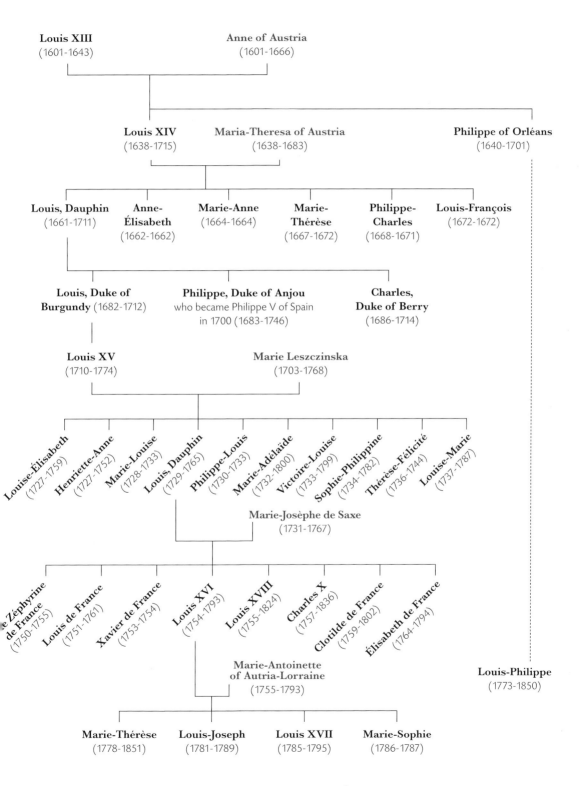

Louis XIII (1601-1643) — Anne of Austria (1601-1666)

Louis XIV (1638-1715) — Maria-Theresa of Austria (1638-1683)

Philippe of Orléans (1640-1701)

Louis, Dauphin (1661-1711)
Anne-Élisabeth (1662-1662)
Marie-Anne (1664-1664)
Marie-Thérèse (1667-1672)
Philippe-Charles (1668-1671)
Louis-François (1672-1672)

Louis, Duke of Burgundy (1682-1712)
Philippe, Duke of Anjou who became Philippe V of Spain in 1700 (1683-1746)
Charles, Duke of Berry (1686-1714)

Louis XV (1710-1774) — Marie Leszczinska (1703-1768)

Louise-Élisabeth (1727-1759)
Henriette-Anne (1727-1752)
Marie-Louise (1728-1733)
Louis, Dauphin (1729-1765)
Philippe-Louis (1730-1733)
Marie-Adélaïde (1732-1800)
Victoire-Louise (1733-1799)
Sophie-Philippine (1734-1782)
Thérèse-Félicité (1736-1744)
Louise-Marie (1737-1787)

Marie-Josèphe de Saxe (1731-1767)

e Zéphyrine de France (1750-1755)
Louis de France (1751-1761)
Xavier de France (1753-1754)
Louis XVI (1754-1793)
Louis XVIII (1755-1824)
Charles X (1757-1836)
Clotilde de France (1759-1802)
Élisabeth de France (1764-1794)

Louis-Philippe (1773-1850)

Marie-Antoinette of Autria-Lorraine (1755-1793)

Marie-Thérèse (1778-1851)
Louis-Joseph (1781-1789)
Louis XVII (1785-1795)
Marie-Sophie (1786-1787)

Établissement public du château, du musée et du domaine national de Versailles

Jean-Vincent Bacquart, head of the publishing department
Marie Leimbacher, Assistant-Head of Publications
Cécile Bouchayer, Head of Publications

Éditions Artlys

Editorial supervision
Séverine Cuzin-Schulte

Editorial coordination
Lucile Desmoulins,
assisted by Annabelle Pegeon

Graphic design
Catherine Enault and Hervé Delemotte

Production
Pierre Kegels

Translation
Ilti

Maps
Thierry Lebreton and Dominique Bissière
Jean-François Péneau

Photo-engraving
Axiome

Printing
Edicolor Print

Unless otherwise stated, all of the works reproduced are housed at the national museum of the Châteaux of Versailles and Trianon.

ISBN: 978-2-85495-530-9
© Établissement public du château, du musée et du domaine national de Versailles, 2013
© Éditions Artlys, Paris, 2013

Printed on February 2016 in Bain-de Bretagne by Edicolor Print
Legal deposit: March 2016